A Working Mom's Guide to Couponing

by
Jennifer Clark

~DEDICATION~

To my loving husband for supporting me in everything I do and to my wonderful kids Nora, Emmy and Ian.

1 CHAPTER- My Story

Would you like to learn how to coupon, but feel that you can't because you work full-time? Do you feel like effective couponing is just too difficult to learn? Couponing doesn't have to be a part-time job, but it can pay off like one! A Working Mom's Guide to Couponing will teach you just how to save money, coupon by cutting corners and provide you the right tools to become an avid coupon shopper.

I started couponing back in February 2011. Couponing couldn't have come at a better time in my life. In January, my husband lost all of his overtime and pay-period deductions had increased greatly by law. Add to that, an increase in healthcare spending due to a couple of diagnosed chronic illnesses and we lost over $15,000 of income within a few months. We needed to drastically cut back on our spending. At that time, our grocery bill was around $800.00 per month. We had to make some major changes and fast. We decided to stop our cable, cut data plans on our cell phones and called our credit cards in order to have lower payments per month. But cutting our bills wasn't enough. The only expense I could control was our grocery bill. In order to reduce our grocery budget that meant I had to buy less at the store. This was hard to do for a family of five, two dogs and one cat.

Shopping at discount stores was a must. Purchasing only generic brands and cutting out luxury food items. Anything over $2.00 was just not in the budget. I had to get creative with lunches and dinners. Fresh fruit and vegetables were only in our home if they were very inexpensive. Even with cutting as much as I did, it still wasn't enough. I was spending on average $150 to $180 per week on food and household products.

I was sick of spending so much money and getting so little. Ironically, on the same night I was frustrated with my grocery bill, my husband and I started watching a show called Extreme Couponing. I was amazed at how much money you can save using coupons! If they could save that much money on groceries, so could I, but how? Where should I start?

I went online the next day and started researching how to coupon. I learned that my original way of couponing was incorrect and I needed to change the way I shop. Several months later, I started saving over 50% of my grocery bill and brought home more food and products than I could ever imagine! I save anywhere from 50% to 90% of my grocery bill every week!

You can save big money, even at drug store chains like Walgreen's, CVS and Rite Aid. You will come to find most of your household products and beauty items can be found for pennies on the dollar at your local drug store. I will explain how to use reward programs, teach you the right combination of coupons and introduce you to rolling your Catalina coupons and Register Rewards. Once you have mastered couponing, you will be able to save at any store. You will never want to purchase products at full price again.

In this economy you can save money and get your family back on track. After one year of couponing, I saved my family $4,800! Couponing can fit into anyone's lifestyle. You just need to know the right tools to succeed. A Full-Time Working Mom's Guide to Couponing can work for anyone who is interested in saving money.

Let's get started!

2 CHAPTER -Working Full-Time

When you first learn how to coupon, you may feel overwhelmed. How can I find time to learn? When am I going to clip and organized all those coupons? Is it worth the time and effort? Working a full-time job can add even more doubts and additional stress.

Once you have the tools and knowledge of how to coupon, the time it takes to put into couponing is well worth the effort. You will be able to run in and out of a grocery store in no time flat with a cart full of groceries, saving 50%! You can have a pantry full of stocked food and products. You will never pay out of pocket for toothpaste, floss, condiments, shampoos, soaps and more! Couponing will change the way you shop.

Working full-time will give you some advantages but also a few disadvantages, but there are ways around those. You might have to work a little bit harder but isn't it worth saving your family $200-$400 per month or more? Not everyone is an extreme couponer and no one really has 40hrs a week to devote to just couponing. I'm going to show you some short cuts to save you time and money. Most important, I want you to understand that couponing doesn't have to control your life.

Getting started, couponing can be frustrating. Start out by learning slowly. On my first shopping trip, I only saved 15% of my total bill. I only had a few coupons to start out with. I was truly disappointed, but I didn't give up. I was expecting huge savings like on the show. As I started couponing more and more each week, I started to understand that I couldn't save exactly like those on Extreme Couponing because I had to purchase milk, eggs, bread, produce and meat.

If you watch the show carefully, you will notice they are only buying 20 items of the same product. If you had 20 coupons and you only bought 20 items of the same product, you're going produce 90% or more in savings. They also speed up the checkout process and don't show you exactly what coupons they are using. The show doesn't reveal to you where they found high-dollar coupons. You just can't find or get coupons for $4.00 off one product. Once you are past the point that Extreme Couponing is just

a show, you will come to understand what true coupon saving is all about.

In the image above, these groceries would have cost $83.00. With coupons, I paid $24.26! I save, on average, 50% or more every time I shop. You can never expect to save 90% to 100% every time you shop. That is just unrealistic. I have saved 80% on a few shopping trips. That is only when shopping for a few specific items on my list. No add-on's like milk, bread, meat and produce. I'm going to teach you how to realistically coupon shop with real savings.

When you start to coupon, you're going to need an online resource. For this full-time working mom I'm going to give you my personal list of coupon blogs I use every day. This list will help you cut corners and save you time and money! In this book I'm going to show you how to start a stockpile. Stockpiling is essential to major coupon savings. The more you have in your stockpile, the less you will need to grocery shop. Instead, you will be shopping for your stockpile. There will be some weeks you won't need to go to the grocery store at all. The less you shop, the more money in your savings. You don't need to have 2 years' worth of products or canned goods shelved in your dining room. You don't need to spend your entire day cutting coupons and getting your grocery list ready for a three hour shopping trip. Your time is valuable. In this book, I want to provide you the right tools to teach you how to coupon smart.

Stop making the excuses and start saving money!

3 CHAPTER -Coupon Terms

In order to understand how to coupon, you need to understand abbreviations and the terms of how coupon. Below I've provided a list of coupon abbreviations you will come across when you begin couponing

$1/2- One dollar off two items
BOGO or B1G1 -Buy One Get One free
B2G1 -Buy Two Get One free
Catalina-The coupons that print off with your receipt
ECB -Extra Care Buck-(CVS cash)
IP- Internet Printable Coupon
DND-Do Not Double
FAR-Free After
GM- General Mills
STACKING-Using stores allow multiple uses of coupons
WYB-When You Buy
CRT-A CVS Store coupon that spits out of the Red Coupon Kiosk
EXP-This is short for expires or expiration date.
IVC-Instant Value Coupon at Walgreen's
MFR or MQ-manufacturer coupon
MIR-Mail in Rebate
MM-money maker…deal where you will make money after coupons are use
ONYO-On Your Next Order
Peelie -Coupon found on the package of a product that can be peelie
OOP -Out of Pocket.
Rain Check-When a store is out of a sale item.
RP-Redplum. Coupon insert that comes in your local paper.
RR- Register Rewards. Catalina from Walgreens.
SS-Smart Source that comes in your local paper.
Tear pad -these are coupons that are on a tear pad usually located on a display or shelf near the item

UPC- The bar code that is scanned to determine pricing
WAGS- Walgreens

You don't need to memorize these abbreviations. You will see them enough in your day to day couponing.

4 CHAPTER List of Coupon Blogs

I'm providing you a list of some popular coupon blogs I have personally used to help me save time and money. Creating shopping lists and coupon match ups take several hours per day. I want to make things easy for you to find blogs in your area that can help.

- Southern Savers-http://www.southernsavers.com/
- Coupon Mom-http://www.couponmom.com/
- I Heart Publix-http://www.iheartpublix.com/
- Savings Cents with Sense-http://www.savingcentswithsense.net/
- I Heart Kroger- http://www.iheartkroger.com/
- Penny Pinching Mom-http://www.pennypinchinmom.com/
- Coupons Dede-http://www.couponsthingsbydede.com/

The list above is blogs located in the southern region of the US. You can fine coupon blogs in every state. There are even coupon blogs that are specific to only one store. Finding a coupon blog close to your home town will help you take advantage of prices in your area. For example, in Florida, Kroger does not double its coupons. You will need to find a coupon blog in Florida to find the best deals for you.

Coupons by Dede is a clipping service. They provide you with a clipping service for your coupons you can buy in bulk. I have used them before and they have fast delivery.

5 CHAPTER How to Use Coupons

I want to start out with the basic way of using a coupon. If you have never used a coupon before, it's pretty simple. You may have a coupon for $0.50 off 1 item. You walk up to the register and hand the cashier your coupon. If your store doubles, you get a total of $1.00 off that item. If you store doesn't double, then you get face value of the coupon.

Before I learned how to coupon, I would clip coupons out of the paper and then head to the store. More times than not, that item was not on sale. Even with that coupon, the generic item next to it was cheaper without a coupon. In the past, I never clipped coupons or even bothered. Why waste all that time clipping coupons when it didn't even lower the price of the item down by half? How do I even know when that item is going to be on sale? That was my old way of thinking. I learned that it wasn't just clipping coupons. I needed to learn when and how to use those coupons. I needed to understand how sale cycles work.

Sale cycles run each month. In order to use your coupon wisely and get top savings you want to use your coupon with a sale item. A typical time frame is 6 to 8 weeks between each sale cycle. Each calendar month brings a new batch of sales. Below is a list of sales cycles run each month.

January: diet foods, super bowl snacks, chips, dips, Coke, Pepsi, Sandwich items, crackers, wings, oranges, pears, Christmas decorations, toys, wrapping papers, cold medicines and vitamins.

February: Canned fruit, pie fillings, vegetables, tuna, canned meats, breakfast items, Eggo waffles, syrup Valentines, chocolate, noodles, and seasonal produce

March: Frozen food month, ice cream, frozen vegetables, meals, waffles, pizza.

April: Ham, eggs, Easter items, baking supplies, organic foods, brownie mix, cake mix, butter, chocolate chips, and spices.

May: BBQ sauce, condiments, charcoal, salad dressing, potato chips, dips, hot dogs, hamburger meat, marinade, salad greens plates, salsa, Memorial Day, Cinco De Mayo, paper products.

June: National Dairy Month, milk, ice cream, cheese, butter, yogurt, whipping cream, cool whip, hot dogs, BBQ sauce, ketchup, charcoal, dips, salad dressing.

August: School supplies, pudding cups, lunch meat, lunchables, bread, cold cereal, waffles, insect repellant, sunscreen, charcoal.

September:. Crayons, pencils, folders, binders, baby items, seasonal produce.

October:. Halloween items, pumpkin, canned pumpkin, baking chips, alarm clocks, batteries, National Seafood month.

November: Hot cocoa, coffee, tea, nuts, chocolate chips, soup, broth, vegetables, Thanksgiving items, turkey, pies, cranberry sauce, Jell-O, marshmallows, stuffing, gravy mixes, potatoes.

December: Holiday dinner, Baking, Canned foods, crackers, soda, ham, cake mix, brownie mix, muffin mix, soup, broth, vegetables.

As you expand your couponing skills you will start to run across a little more complicated coupons and scenarios. Stacking coupons is the best way to maximize your savings. Stacking is combining a store coupon with a manufacture coupon, per one item. Try not to confuse the terms doubling with stacking. Doubling coupons means the store is taking the value of the coupon and doubling it.

In order to stack your coupons, you need to make sure you have a store coupon. Just because a store logo or name is on the coupon, doesn't make it store coupon. Many store coupons can have barcodes on them. You want to check and make sure it's a true store coupon and not a manufacture coupon.

In this image you have a Kroger store coupon. The first noticeable indication is this coupon has written at the top "Store Coupon". There is no bar code at the bottom of the coupon. This coupon is valid only at Kroger.

In this example, this store coupon has a barcode on it. On the top of the coupon it states "Store Coupon". This means that this coupon is valid only at Albertsons.

In this next example, this coupon looks exactly like the Kroger store coupon. If you look closely, you will see that this coupon is a manufacturer coupon and NOT a Store coupon. You can use this coupon at any grocery chain that allows Kroger coupons and use it as a manufacture coupon. It's very important when stacking coupons to read over all the fine print and terms listed on your coupon.

You may find a coupon that has $1.00 off 3 items. Can you combine other coupons with that coupon since you have 3 items? The term "one coupon per item" comes to mind.

The answer is no. Let me explain further.
The Swanson coupon reads $1.00 off 3 Swanson broth or stock cartons or Swanson Flavor Boost broth. This means you need to buy 3 of those items to get the $1.00 off. If you attempt to use your $1.00/3 coupon and only buy 2 items, your coupon will be rejected. You cannot combine another Swanson broth manufacture coupon with the one above. BUT, you can combine a store coupon.

The reason why you cannot use another manufacture coupon with the 2 other broths is because all three broths are attached to that UPC barcode. We will go into more detail about barcodes in another section of this book.

If your store allows stacking, then you will be able to combine a store coupon with that manufacture coupon. If you have a store coupon for $1.00/1 Swanson Broth item, then you can use 3 store coupons and your $1.00/3 manufacture coupon to get the best discount.

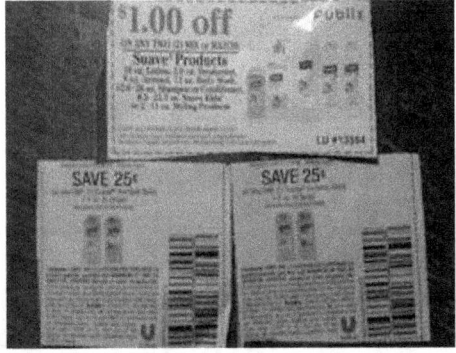

In the image above you have two manufacture coupons for Suave Invisible Solid and one store coupon for $1.00 off any 2 mix or match suave products. This gives you a good visual of stacking coupons

Coupons with "one coupon per transaction" means you are only allowed to use that coupon once at checkout. You cannot stack or use the same coupon again in the same transaction. Coupons like these are usually large dollar coupons such as $5.00 off your purchase of $30.00 or more. You will need to purchase $30.00 worth of groceries in order to use that coupon at checkout. You can do several transactions at one time if you have several of these coupons. You just need to split your groceries totalling up to $30.00. Let the cashier know you are making two or three transactions and use the divider bar if necessary.

Make sure to check your receipt before you leave the store to make sure you received the discount. The term "Limit of 4 like Coupons in same shopping trip" is common with P&G coupons. This means you are only allowed to use those four same coupons in that transaction. Restrictions are listed by the manufacture to help cut back on low stock and empty shelves or restricting the number of high value coupons at once. In some cases, managers or cashiers will allow you to use more than what is stated on the coupon. If you do use more than what is stated on the coupon your coupon may get rejected at the register. If you plan ahead and divide your shopping trips into different transactions, you can maximize your savings!

Use competitor coupons with your manufacture coupons. Check your local stores coupon policy and you might be surprised to find out they take other store coupons! My Publix allows Target, Kroger and Whole Food coupons. These coupons are considered "store coupons".

Which means you can combine them with your manufacture coupons. Wal- Mart doesn't allow competitor coupons but they match competitor sales. Bring in your Kroger sales flier and they will match that sale price.

Lastly, use your coupons in order. Present your $5.00 off $20.00 coupon first. This way your total savings does not go below the total purchase price. Next hand the cashier all your coupons that offer FREE products. This makes it easier for the cashier to track down the free items first. They need to look up that price and enter in the amount. Next you hand the cashier all your manufacture and store coupons. I keep all like coupons together. This makes it easier for you and cashier when checking out. With time and practice you will fully understand how to use your coupons wisely and coupon like a pro!

6 CHAPTER- BOGO Sales

I have to tell you, I love BOGO sales. BOGO means Buy One, Get One Free. Many stores run BOGO sales and depending on your stores policy you can grab some pretty good deals. Many stores accept a manufacture coupon and a store coupon. Some stores accept competitor coupons and some do not. This all depends on the coupon policy at each store. Stores like Rite Aid, Walgreens & CVS allow you to use a BOGO Coupon on a BOGO Sale getting 2 items for FREE. BOGO sales and BOGO coupons can get complicated, but I've broken it down for you in each scenario.

BOGO SALE SENERIO 1:
You buy 1 Old El Paso Dinner Kit, BOGO $3.19 ($1.59) <----HALF OFF PRICE
-$0.50/1 Old El Paso Product (SS 5/12) <---This was the coupon used for this deal
You Pay- $0.59 for 1 Old El Paso Dinner Kit<-----What you pay out of pocket with coupon.

With the first scenario, you can pick up one dinner kit very cheap. You do not need to buy 2 items for a BOGO sale to work. The ONLY time you need to buy two items on a BOGO sale is if the coupon you are using requires you to buy two products.

BOGO SALE SENERIO 2:
You buy 2 Lysol Cleaning Spray BOGO at $3.99 ($1.99) <---HALF OFF PRICE
-$0.50/1 Lysol Cleaning Spray (SS 2/12) <---Use 2 Manufacture Coupons
-$1.00 Lysol Cleaning Spray Store Coupon<-----Use 2 Store Coupons
You Get Both FREE<----What you pay out of pocket with coupon

In Scenario 2 you have more coupons you can use to buy more products on sale. Here you can use 2 $0.50 manufacture coupons and use 2 $1.00 off store coupons for each products. (Remember its one manufacture coupon and one store coupon per item!) The $0.50 manufacture coupon doubles to a $1.00 and the store coupon is a face value giving you $2.00 off each product. You Get Both Lysol Cleaning Sprays for FREE.

BOGO SALE SENERIO 3:

You buy 2 Dole Pineapple Juice BOGO at $1.99 ($0.99) <---HALF OFF PRICE
-$0.50/2 Dole Pineapple Juice (SS 2/12) <------Use 1 Manufacture Coupon
You Pay-$0.99 for 2 juices with the coupon<----What you pay out of pocket with coupon

In Scenario 3, you have one coupon. You NEED to buy 2 Dole Pineapple Juices to get the $0.50 off. If your store doubles that makes your $0.50 coupon now worth $1.00. You can't take one pineapple juice to the register and use the coupon. The coupon will be rejected.

BOGO coupons are manufactures coupon that allows you to buy one item and get it free. A BOGO coupon you can use with a BOGO sale IF your store allows it. You need to check with your stores policy before you use a BOGO coupon with a BOGO sale. You are only allowed to purchase two products with the BOGO sale and BOGO coupon. Many couponers ask if you can use a $1.00/1 manufacture coupons with a BOGO coupon. This is where things can get a little tricky. The answer is yes and no. First you need to determine if the BOGO Coupon attaches to 1 of the 2 products you are buying or if it attaches to both of the products you are buying. To figure this out you need to look at the barcode on the coupon.

BOGO deals are usually coded with (14), (00) or (01). These codes are located in the Value code area. If the numbers are (00) or (01) – then the coupon only attaches to the product you are getting for free and another coupon can be used against the other product. If the numbers are (14) – The coupon attaches to both products and you CAN NOT use another coupon. Any additional coupons used will beep.

BOGO COUPON SENERIO 1- COUPON BAR CODE 00 or 01

Buy (1) Lysol Cleaning Spray $1.99
Buy (1) Lysol Cleaning Dust Rags $2.99
-Use Buy One Lysol Cleaning Spray Get One Lysol Dust Rag FREE Coupon (coupon attaches to spray)
-Use $1.00/1 Lysol Cleaning Dust Rag coupon with the BOGO Coupon. (Attaches to the Dust Rag)

When you go to check out the Dust Rag product will be free ($2.99). Since the coupon for the free dust rag is attached to the spray you can use the $1.00 off coupon for the dust rag, making your total purchase $0.99 for the dust rag and spray.

BOGO COUPON SENERIO 2 – COUPON BAR CODE 14

Buy (2) Lysol Cleaning Sprays
-Use Buy One Lysol Cleaning Spray Get One Lysol Spray FREE coupon

Since the bar code above is (14) you cannot attach another manufacture coupon to the BOGO coupon. The Bar code attaches to both products. If you tried to use another manufacture coupon the register would reject it. (Remember-you can use a store coupon in this scenario!)

I know with all these bar code numbers your starting to think "Do I have to look at EVERY bar code on EVERY BOGO coupon?" The answer is no. A good rule of thumb is if the BOGO coupon shows two of the same product (Buy One Lysol Cleaning Spray Get One Lysol Spray) you most likely cannot use another coupon with that BOGO coupon. If the BOGO coupon states you buy one product you get a different product FREE (Buy One Lysol Cleaning Spray Get One Lysol Duster) then you can most likely use another product coupon for that free item.

Can you use two BOGO coupons together making both items FREE? I personally never used BOGO coupons this way and I believe many stores do not allow it.

You can however do this scenario:
Buy 4 Reach toothbrushes at $2.50
-Use (2) BOGO coupons
-Use (2) $1/1 coupons
Final Price: $2.50 for all 4 items.

That scenario should be fine providing those Reach coupons don't have a "14" in the value code.

What about 50% off sales using a BOGO coupon? This can be tricky. It depends on the stores coupon policy. Drug stores like Walgreen and Rite Aid typically do this type of sale. In this case you buy one item at full price and get the second at 50% off. If you have a BOGO coupon, the value of the lowest priced item is the one that should be applied to the coupon. So here is a sample scenario:

Buy 1 Gillette body wash at $4.99 Get one 50% off at $2.49
-Use BOGO coupon (should take off $2.49)
Final Price: $4.99

There might be some situations where a cashier takes off the higher priced item, but in general these almost never work out to be a very good deal. You can always try. The worst case is the cashier tells you no.

7 CHAPTER Decoding UPC Codes

In this chapter, I want to go into further detail decoding UPC code. As you may have noticed, there are two UPC codes. One is the UPC and the other is the GS1 Data bar. Soon enough the UPC symbol will be replaced with the GS1 Data bar. The new data bar is to provide more options to the manufacturers. They can offer more complex offers, more options for purchase requirements and values, reduce fraudulent coupon used and have better scanning accuracy. It will also be able to allow retailers to code chain-specific promotions, which has been impossible to do until now. It will also improve tracking and auditing back to the manufacturers.

Anatomy of a Barcode

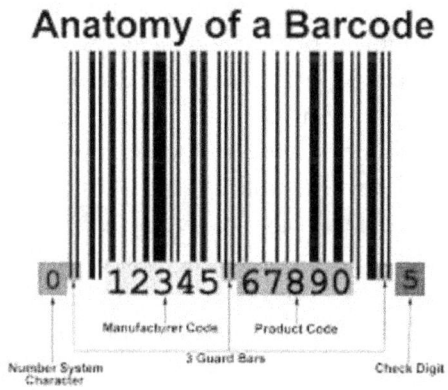

Coupon UPC codes are made up of five sections with a total of 12 numbers. Each section is used to match up products and to the value of the coupon. All coupons should begin with the number 5, which is called the NSC or Number System Character. Next there is a five digit (12345 above) manufacturer number.

This number should match the manufacturer number on the product. The next set of three numbers (678) is called the family code. This code is used to verify that the shopper has purchased the product which applies to the coupon. The two numbers which follow the family code is called the value code. This determines the value of the coupon. The two numbers which follow the family code is called the value code. This determines the value of the coupon. The final number is called a check digit. All UPC numbers contain a check digit which is automatically calculated based on the previous numbers on the UPC symbol.

The first digit of the manufacturer's identification number is special. It is called the number system character. The code will be 5 or 9 when using a grocery store coupon. If a coupon begins with a 5, this tells the register that the coupon can be doubled. If the code begins with a 9, this tells the register that the coupon cannot double. Sometimes you will see a coupon with the "Do Not Double" at the top but it has the number 5 in the bar code below. If the coupon is scanned it will double at stores that allow doubling. The cashier will have to override this. The grocery chain pays for the doubled amount – not the manufacturer. It is at the discretion of the store as to whether or not to double the coupon.

The manufacturer will never pay for the doubling. Many of the coupons you find with the number 9 on them are in store coupons such as peelies. If you use a coupon with the number 9 it may cause the cash register to beep, even if the coupon matches the product. Remember that the cash register beeping or not beeping does not indicate improper usage. So don't be scared when the cash register beeps at you.

The following data below shows you what different number system characters mean:

0 = Standard UPC number (must have a zero to do zero-suppressed numbers)

1=Reserved

2 = Random-weight items (fruits, vegetables, meats, etc.) 3 = Pharmaceuticals

4 = In-store marketing for retailers (A store can set up its own code, but no other store will understand them.)

5=Coupons

6 = Standard UPC number

7=Standard UPS number

8=Reserved

9=Reserved

This code tells the computer that to take a $1.00 off one item

'The value code, tells the cash register what the coupon is worth. In this image above the coupon is worth $1.00.

If you see a coupon with 00 on the bar code that means the cashier has to manually input the coupon value. The code 01 means Free and 02 means Buy 4 get 1 Free (same product). Value codes are helpful to know how many coupons you can use.

Remember, you can only use one manufacturer coupon per item. This does not mean that you can always use one actual coupon per item.

The value code tells the computer how many items it must scan in order for the coupon to be valid. It "attaches" to each of these bar codes. For instance, if you have a coupon that states $1.00/2 X brand products this means the coupon will attach itself to 2 X brands. You will not be able to use another manufacture coupon. So, you may have 20 items, you can use 10 $1.00/2 coupons, making all of your items attached to those coupons.

The next important set of numbers (678 in our example) is the family code. A set of 3 digits with no zeroes at the end means that the coupon is good for a specified variety of the product. If there were one zero at the end then the coupon would be good for more than one variety of that product. If there were 2 zeroes at the end then the coupon would be good for more than one type of that product.

For example, 678 would mean the coupon is good ONLY for an 8 count box of Brand X granola bars. If you see 670, that would mean the coupon would probably work on any flavor of Brand X granola bars and most likely any size. Next is 600 would mean the coupon would probably work on just about any type of cereal, granola bars or food products that Brand X sells.

When decoding your coupon remember that this is for educational purposes only. Using the coupon bar code to "cheat the register" is considered fraudulent. Bar code decoders try using high value coupons on a smaller or inexpensive product from the same brand but which is NOT listed on the coupon, thus getting it for free or with overage.

Bar codes are a good practice to read and understand when an item is on sale and you have a coupon for that product. You want to make sure the sales tag on the shelf matches the products bar code. You want to avoid purchasing the wrong product, such as "low sodium" product not being included in the sale with your coupon. Understanding bar codes is not a necessity in learning how to coupon, but it is helpful to know how your coupon works.

8 CHAPTER -Catalina Coupons

Catalina coupons are essential to better coupon savings. What is a Catalina coupon? Catalina coupons are printed at the register at participating stores when you purchase select participating items. Many drug and grocery stores will print out Catalina coupons after you've purchased your items at that store. Your sale triggers new coupons to print for your next purchase. Many of the Catalina coupons that are printed are manufacture coupons that can be used at other stores. If your Catalina has a bar code for a manufacturer coupon (starting with 5 or 9) you may be able to use it at another store.

There are several types of Catalina coupons. When you purchase a particular product it may print out a coupon for a competitor's product. You may even receive a Catalina store coupon for $3.00 of your next purchase at that particular store. Other Catalina coupons may not even be coupons at all, but advertisements. To make sure your Catalina is a coupon look for the bar code.

Many Catalina coupons are based on shelf price. Shelf price is the amount of the item before the sale price. For example, in order for you to print your Catalina coupon you need to purchase $12.00 of product X. The product is on sale for $3.00. The regular "shelf price" is $4.00. You need to purchase 3 of those products in order to get the Catalina sale. This all depends on your store. Some base Catalina coupons on the sale price

Can you role Catalina Coupons? Rolling means – can you purchase a Catalina deal and use a Catalina from the prior transaction – and still get another Catalina. Many Catalina's will roll. Check the rules on bottom of the Catalina.

How can I found out about Catalina deals? Many drug stores will advertise Catalina deals on their weekly flier. You can find some of them on Coupon Network. You may even get notices that will print out of the Catalina machine giving you notice of upcoming Catalina deals.

What if your Catalina didn't print? There can be many reasons for it not to print such as you didn't purchase the right amount of product. Even if you missed it by a penny the Catalina will not print. The machine could be out of paper. The Catalina deal ended. The particular size you purchased was not part of the Catalina deal. Always double check and make sure you have the right size, price and date for your Catalina coupons to print. If there is a glitch in the machine and you purchased every item correct you can always contact customer service. The store will help you solve the situation and more than likely give you a refund.

The Coupon Network by Catalina is a great website to find your Catalina deals. They give you a list of products on sale and let you know how many you need to purchase in order to print your Catalina coupon. This is a great tool to use when checking out. You can do several transactions to max out your savings.

Transaction #1:
Buy 5 Kraft Salad Dressing $1.99 (total $9.95 before coupons)
-(2) $1.25/2 Kraft Salad Dressing
-(1)$.75/1 Printable Kraft Printable Kraft Paid: $ $6.70
Received a $5.00 Catalina

Transaction #2:
Buy 4 Ragu -$2.25 (total $9.00 before coupons) Buy 1 Country Crock-total ($1.75 before coupons)
-(2)$1/2 Ragu
-(1)$.50/1 Country Crock (doubles) Total: $7.75
Use $5.00 Catalina from previous transaction Pay: $2.75
Receive a $5.00 Catalina]

Transaction #3:
Buy 10 Hunts Tomatoes (total $7.70) Buy 12 La Yogurt (total$3.48)
-(3) $.45/3 Hunts
-(1) $1.50/12 La Yogurt
-(1) $.25 La Yogurt (store coupon usually don't double)
Total: $6.73
Use $5.00 Catalina from previous transaction Pay: $1.73

No Catalina for this deal. However you could have rolled this as many times as you had coupons for. I paid out of pocket $11.18 for $65.78 worth of groceries.

Rolling Catalina coupons can be difficult for a beginner couponer. Many coupon blogs will offer such transactions for you to try and do on your own. As long as you have the patience and basic coupon knowledge you can accomplish rolling Catalina's.

9 CHAPTER -How to Find Coupons

When you're not looking for coupons you really don't see them. When you are looking for coupons they are everywhere! Some are hidden, some are out in the open and some are in places you are familiar with. First, the most obvious spot is your local Sunday paper. Every Sunday, except holiday week, you can find coupon inserts in your local paper.

The general rule is one coupon per person in your home. This depends on how many people are in your family. I purchase about 2-4 Sunday papers each week. You want as many of the same coupon because you're going to start building a stock pile. This is how you're going to save money on top of saving at the grocery store. Some papers will have a store coupon for "$10.00 off your $50.00 purchase" in an odd section of the paper.

Make sure to look through the inside of your paper and not just pull inserts out. I currently live in Cobb County, which is great because they hand out the AJC nightly Thursday paper for FREE on my front lawn. It's not a full insert but it still has some great coupons and it's free. Check any odd papers; you never know if you'll find coupons inside. Check your local grocery stores and drug stores. Publix, Kroger, BJ's Wholesale, Target, Rite Aid, CVS and Walgreen's have store coupons which are valuable. Store coupons can be combined with manufacture coupons. This gives you maximum savings on one item.

Kroger has online e-coupons you can load onto your Kroger card. You can sign up as a member and load your coupons for free! Kroger also tracks what you buy and sends you coupon books in the mail

I have pets and buy pet food, so stores send me coupon booklets with pet coupons inside. When you sign up make sure to list your current address. Currently, I have about 4 to 5 Kroger coupon books come from the mail. They also send you bonus coupons for FREE items too!

Publix also has coupon books that you can find either right when you walk in or at the customer service desk. Just ask for the latest coupon book besides the yellow advantage and the green advantage flier. Some coupon books require you on a website before they get mailed to you. Publix also has a baby program that is awesome! They will send you free items, coupons and more. Just go to their website and sign up for all their programs. Check the customer service desk at your favorite store and see what store coupons they may have. If you can't find many coupons in your area or you live in a rural area too far to pick up a city paper, don't worry you can still get coupons!

You can purchase coupons online. There are many websites that offer coupon clipping services to clip single coupons or mail out whole coupon inserts to your home. This is a wonderful service if you only have say one or two coupons for a great sale coming up and you want to stockpile that item. When I see a good deal coming up and I want 10 or more of those items, I head online to purchase my coupons. Coupons get mailed out to my home usually days before the sale.

When purchasing coupons you feel you will use in the future, make sure the expiration date is far enough ahead. You don't want to purchase coupons that will expire in less than a week and then never use them.

I also receive coupon inserts from friends and family. My mother-in law gives me her unused coupons. I have co-workers that will also bring in unwanted coupon inserts. You will be surprise at how many people are willing to let go of those coupons. This works out great for me when some weekends I'm so busy or I have to work and I can't go out and buy my Sunday paper. I still have coupons I can use.

Printable coupons are easy to find and print right at home. Coupons found online sometimes are not in your local paper. Manufactures place coupons on websites like Coupons.com, Redplum.com, SmartSource.com and your favorite brands websites. If you are a Facebook fan, you can also get coupons on Facebook. I highly recommend opening a Facebook page just for coupons. Manufacturing companies are heading to Facebook and providing special saving coupons if you like them on your Facebook page.

When printing your coupons, only print what you think you will use or when you have your shopping list. You can waste a lot of paper and ink printing coupons you will never use.

Another way you can receive some valuable coupons is to contact your favorite product company. Email or write them a letter telling them how much you enjoy and use their product. Give them examples, the more detailed the better. If you are unhappy, let them know as well and tell them why you are unhappy. If you take the time to write the letter many times they will write back to you with great valuable coupons, sometimes for FREE products.

What works best is to tell them your honest opinion. Don't just write them a letter asking for coupons. You might not get a response back. Keep a list of all the companies you contacted and what types of coupons they sent you. This way you won't write the same company twice (many products run under the same big corporation such as Nestle or General Mills) and in 4 to 6 weeks you can write that company again about another product.

As mentioned above those are the main sources where I collect coupons.

There are other sources like dumpster diving, coupon trains, magazines, binkies in your store isle, inside samples you receive, cash registers (Catalina coupons) and inside product boxes. Coupons are everywhere.

10 CHAPTER- How to Organize Coupons

Organizing your coupons doesn't take up as much time as you think if you have a plan in place. Sunday afternoon or when my son is taking a nap is the best time for me to cut and organize my coupons. Try to pick a time when it's quite, grab a cup of coffee or tea and just sit down at your dining room table. Choose a large space to spread out your coupon inserts. You are going to make separate piles that you can easily reach. I organize my fliers into piles of Red Plum, Smart Source and P&G according to dates. I might have several weeks of Sunday coupon inserts that I didn't get to the past Sunday. Just try to get to them when you can.

I start to grab the first pile of coupon inserts and rip each page out and place them on the table or floor into "like" piles. If there are coupons on the front and back that I'm not going to use, just throw them away. Once I have everything ripped out, I then start cutting my coupons. I don't cut each coupon out. I take the small pile, usually 4 like pages and cut them all at the same time. This trick saves me time cutting. Once the coupons are cut, I place them on my kitchen table in piles according to my coupon book. One pile for condiments, one pile for freezer, one pile for laundry until I have all my coupons cut and organized into small piles around me.

I then open my coupon binder and insert all my coupons. If I notice any expired coupons, this is when I take them out. Expired coupons are usually in the middle of the month and the end of the month. (Example 12/15/12 and 12/31/12). You can either throw out your expired coupons or donate them to families in the military. They can use expired coupons up to 6 months after the expiration date. Check your local area military base if they are accepting coupons or you can just go online and search.

Another way couponers organized their coupons is by Accordion File Method. I personally do both when I don't have time to cut my coupons. The accordion file method offers less cutting, but a larger storage method. You can purchase any 13 file accordion folder at your local office store. Start out by collecting your first weeks of coupon inserts and placing them in one folder. It's good to write the date on the front page of the insert for quick reference. You can find the date of your coupon insert in fine print on the side of the insert binder. The following week inserts in the next file and so forth.

When you are ready to get coupons together, you pull out the insert you need and clip only the coupons you want. Many of the blogs will tell you where the coupon is located to find them. (SS 2/12), Smart Source, February 2012 edition. This method is great for cutting back time, but you won't be able to easily grab coupons for on the go sales. You will also need a bi- fold or envelope to keep your loose coupons such as printable coupons, Catalina and binkies. There is no wrong or right way to keep your coupons. You just need to find a way that works best for you.

When I go shopping, I don't usually bring my binder with me. I keep my coupons in a coupon holder. This can be a small envelope or a small coupon bi-fold you buy at the store. I keep all of my coupons in my bi- fold while shopping so I have less to carry in the store. My coupons are already pulled out and matched with my shopping list and I can just hand them to the cashier when it's time to check out. My binder is also safe at home. I won't lose my binder at the store or have someone walk out of the store with my binder. I view my binder like money. It has hundreds of dollars' worth of coupons I worked hard to find and organize.

I love using my bi-fold because it cuts my shopping trip in half. If you bring your binder and you don't have your coupons pulled you are then standing off to the side of the isle digging and digging for coupons. This full-time working mom doesn't have time to dig. She needs to grab her numbered items off her list and head to the register. I know how many coupons I already have, ready to go. Plus you just jumped in head of that lady digging for her coupons to grab your items first.

Of course, be courteous and don't grab the five last items off the shelf. I'm always nice and ask if she wanted to purchase this item as well. Inside my bi-fold I keep all product coupons together. If you have a store coupon and a manufacture coupon for the same product, keep them together. Next, you want to place any FREE items in the front of your pile. Those FREE items need to be on the checkout belt or handed to the cashier first. This will help your cashier find those FREE items fast with those coupons and they will be very thankful for your organization skills.

As you shop, you may find that some of the items are gone or not priced on sale per your list. Just simply pull those coupons out of your pile. Cashiers like couponers to be organized and ready. This way you don't hold up the line and the customers behind you doesn't get upset. You can organize your coupons to what works best for you.

11 CHAPTER- How to Make a Coupon Binder

Creating a coupon binder is relatively easy. I love my binder and love how easy it is to find the coupons I need fast for my shopping list. There is no right or wrong way to make a coupon binder. I've provided for you some simple steps to create a binder
What you need:

* A binder (3" or 5" binder)
* Coupons
* Baseball card pages
* Covers
* Dividers
* Folders
* Scissors

Once you have everything listed above you can then decide how to list your categories by type. In my coupon binder I have

Snacks, Sweets, Condiments, Baking, Fridge, Frozen, Breakfast, Prepared Sides, Soup, Fruit, Vegetables, Drinks, Yogurt, Baby, Laundry, Cleaning Supplies, Pasta, Paper Products, Dish Washing, Air Fresheners, Medicine, First Aid, Oral Care, Hair Care, Beauty/Makeup, Soap, Shaving, Deodorant, Feminine Hygiene, Pets, and Misc.:

You can find all kinds of creative coupon binder covers, holders and unique ways to use your binder in stores. Just do a search online! When you have finished making your coupon binder be sure to have copies of all your coupon policies and place them in one of the folders or side pockets for easy access.

Add a folder to hold all of the current weekly sales fliers (if your binder has pockets on the inside of the cover, you can use those instead). Keep a pen and scissors handy as well. You never know when you need to clip a coupon out of a flier in your local grocery store. Organization is necessary to having a faster and more efficient shopping trip!

Working moms know we have limited time on our hands!

12 CHAPTER-Change the Way you Shop

Now that you've clipped your coupons and have your coupons safely stored in your binder, you are ready to start shopping. First and foremost you need to be open minded when trying new products. Coupons come out all the time to let consumers try out new products. Sometimes you find great deals and discover products you like. Other times the product isn't worth purchasing. It's up to you and your family what products you want to use and purchase.

I currently have 2-3 different laundry soaps that I purchase for my home. If say Wisk has a great coupon, I'll be more than happy to buy Wisk at a lower sale price that week then Tide or Gain. This goes for all products you buy. If you or a family members only like a particular brand, then when that coupon comes out make sure to really stockpile on that product. This will save you money in the long run.

Before I started couponing, I always bought generic or store brand items because it was cheaper. Sometimes the store brand was just as good as name brand, but most of the time the quality just wasn't as great. Now when I shop, I only buy name brand items because it's much cheaper than the store brand.

When you put together your grocery list, you are making a list of what is on sale at the lowest price. This is going to be your stockpile items. Once you have your stock up list, you can then add items you need like meat, dairy, fruits and veggies. Many coupon blogs will give you an indication of what is a good deal to stock up on. I use several coupon blogs that already have a list of everything on sale. As a working mom, I don't have time to match coupons with sales.

This takes a tremendous amount of time. Many of these blogs are run by stay at home moms who love to coupon and have the time to create lists for you. They match the coupons you need for each sale item. All you have to do is find that coupon in your coupon binder

A good general rule is anything under $1.00 is a good stock up price. Once you have about three to six months of coupon shopping under your belt, you will get an idea of what is a good stock up price. Many blogs already have "stock-up" lists made for you. Remember every city has different prices for different areas and what's one person's stock-up price may not be for another.

I provided an image of the shopping (last page of this chapter) I use from a coupon blogger site. As you can see, the blogger site has organized the list by BOGO sale items and prices. This blogger uses an acorn as her "stock up" price indicator. The letter (M) indicates manufacture coupon. The letter (S) is for store coupon. You can also print the coupon you need for that sale item. Just click on the link and print your coupon. Another way to find your coupon is by this symbol. (SS 12/01) That indicates the coupon is from your Smart Source insert week of December 1st.

With the same list, write down how many items you need to purchase. Next to the Kellogg's cereal I put the number 3. I know that when I'm shopping to grab 3 boxes of Kellogg cereal. The check mark I made is next to the coupon I have to use and give to the cashier. I have 3 $0.50/1 Kellogg Frosted Flakes cereal coupon. Those coupons will likely double, making them $1.00 off. The product is on sale BOGO, making Kellogg cereal $2.14. I will likely pay $1.14 for each box.

When you're shopping sometimes you won't be able to find that coupon for that stock-up product. Generally if I don't have that coupon, I don't buy it. If I need that product and I don't have a coupon, then I go for the generic item. Don't worry if you don't have that coupon, the item will go on sale again. The main reason you are shopping only sale items is to build your stockpile and lower your overall grocery bill. The goal is to build your stockpile to the point where you won't need to purchase those items for 4 to 6 weeks, thus cutting down your shopping list. Soon enough you will only need perishable items on your list that you can't stockpile.

Your grocery bill will get lower and lower each month. I'm now to the point I only spend $50.00 to $80.00 per week on my family for groceries. My home is full of healthy food, frozen chicken and meats, soups, canned vegetables and broth, spaghetti noodles and sauce. Your stockpile doesn't have to look like a grocery store inside your home.

Your Shopping List Printed from
Bloggers Website

◄ View Post

Coupons for Publix Ad

1/2-1/8 (1/3-1/9)

Clip 'n
Saze

Buy One Get Ones

🏠 ⊕ ⊕

Armour Meatballs, 14 oz, (price not listed) **Regional Deal** ✂
- -$1/2 Armour frozen meatballs PRINTABLE ▣

Hormel Country Crock Side Dishes, 20-24 oz, at $3.99 ($1.99) ✂

Your coupon --> -$1 off Hormel Country Crock side dish
PRINTABLE ▣
(makes it 99¢)

Kozy Shack Pudding Bread, Tapicoca, Rice, or Chocolate, 4-6 ct., or 22 oz, at $3.19 ($1.59) ✂

Quaker Cereal, 14.5-18 oz, at $4.89 ($2.44) ✂
Life or Oatmeal Squares
- -$1/2 Quaker products, January All You magazine
- -$1/2 Quaker products PRINTABLE ▣
(makes it $1.94 ea.)

The nut indicates
stock up price -->
🌰 **Kellogg's Cereal, 10.5-14.7 oz, at $4.29 ($2.14)** ✂
Frosted Flakes. Chocolate Frosted Flakes. Krave, or
Corn Pops
- -$1/2 Kellogg's cereals, 8.7 oz+ PRINTABLE ▣
- - 50/1 Kellogg's Frosted Flakes cereal printable (limit reached)
- -$1/2 Kellogg's cereals, 10 oz + printable (limit reached)
- -$1/2 Kellogg's Frosted Flakes cereals, 14 oz+ (Facebook) PRINTABLE ▣
- - 70/1 Kellogg's Frosted Flakes Choco Zucaritas cereal, 14.7 oz + PRINTABLE ▣
- - 70/1 Kellogg's Krave cereal, 11 oz + PRINTABLE ▣
- - 50/1 Kellogg's Frosted Flakes cereal, 14 oz+ PRINTABLE ▣
- -$1/2 Kellogg's Frosted Flakes. Krave. Froot Loops Corn Pops, Apple Jacks, Frosted Mini Wheats Little Bites. or Honey Smacks cereal PRINTABLE ▣
- - 50/1 Kellogg's Krave cereal. 11 oz+ PRIN
- -$1/2 Kellogg's Corn Pops cereals. 9.2 o

13 CHAPTER Tackling the Stores

Once you have your coupon match-up list completed and your coupons ready, you are ready to tackle the stores. When you first start to coupon, start slow and shop only one or two stores you are comfortable with. This way you won't get overwhelmed learning all the different coupon policies for each store. Every store has its own way of handling coupons. Managers have the right to refuse or take coupons aside of the coupon policy. You want to see how well the cashiers know the coupon policy and if they are coupon friendly. Most stores have a copy of their coupon policy posted out front or have a printed policy you can have at Customer Service. Keep that with you at all times in case your cashier is new. Always be polite and don't argue with the managers.

You will soon learn who your favorite cashiers are and who you tend to avoid. Each store has its own unique way of saving you money. Wither its coupon books, eCoupons, BOGO sales, doubling or tripling coupons, you need to check out your store.

Watch your cashier when they start to scan your coupons. Sometimes your coupons will stick together, don't double, miss-scanned or get dropped on the floor. Just kindly note to the cashier and they will correct it. Check out your limits of "like" coupons in each store.

Kroger, where I shop, only allows 4 like coupons per item. This means I can only use 4 coupons with the 4 items I buy. They don't have a limit on total coupons, but they don't want you clearing the shelves with 20 bottles of mustard. The Publix where I shop doesn't seem to have a limit, but I have never bought over 8 total items

I never clear shelves and make sure that other couponers have the opportunity to buy that item as well. If you have 20 coupons that you want to use, go to two different stores if you can or come back on two different days. Best case, you can call ahead and pre-order your items. This way, everyone has a chance at that awesome coupon deal.

Try to shop the stores early or even late in the evening. If you can shop at the beginning of the sale you have the best chance to get everything on your list. This doesn't always happen if you work full-time or work odd hours of the day. If they are out of an item, don't panic, you can always get a rain check on that item and come back when it's in stock. If you tend to shop in the late evening, you can have a nicer shopping trip with less customers standing behind you when you have a handful of coupons.

Grocery stores tend to restock in the evening. Items out of stock during the day will get restocked in the evening, giving you another chance to grab that hot coupon item. Last but not least, make sure you are not hungry when you shop! Remember, you are trying to save money and the stores can easily tempt you with yummy bakery items, tasty samples and delicious treats to get you to purchase items that you may not have a coupon for. Stick to your list and keep only the coupons you want to use with you. I keep my binder at home for that reason. Even though I may see an awesome deal not on my list, I don't have my coupon binder with me. If I really want that item I'll come back later to get it. This keeps my grocery total budget low and more money in my pocket!

14 CHAPTER Starting your Stockpile

Your stockpile is essential to you saving BIG money at the cash register. First, I want to define what a stockpile is. A stockpile is a collection of products that you have purchased that can be used to get your family through to the next sales cycle.

Why is it important to have a stockpile?
It's simple. When you find a product at its lowest price you want to buy as much as you can and stock up for at least 6-8 weeks. This is the typical length of any sales cycle. When you have plenty of toilet tissue in your stockpile to last 6 to 8 weeks, you can cross off that item on your grocery list.

Once you start to add up everything in your stockpile, before you know it, you're only buying disposable items like milk, eggs, meats, veggies and fruit. Stockpiling is the main part of couponing. Without your stockpile, you won't be able to lower your weekly or monthly budget by half or more.

When building your stockpile you want to purchase items that are only at rock bottom prices. You do not want to spend extra money per week building your stockpile. Your stockpile will slowly build over time with the more deals your find. If you start to spend more per week than you normally do, you are defeating the purpose of building a stockpile. Purchase items you know your family will use. It's a waste of money to buy candy bars you know your family will never eat. If you plan to purchase cat treats and you don't have a cat, but because it's free, donate the cat treats to your local shelter. There is no reason to keep cat treats you will never use in a stockpile. Another rule I use when building my stockpile is, when I see a good deal on a product and I don't know if my family will like it, I purchase only a few of those items.

If my family truly loves the new product, I then go back with the rest of my coupons and purchase enough for my stockpile. Soon enough, you will get to know everything in your stockpile. I know my family loves pickles, so every time there is a great sale on them I make sure to grab 10 or more jars of pickles. Sometimes I buy more than 6 to 8 weeks' worth.

Once you've started a pretty good stockpile, where to do you put it all? I've seen people get creative and put them in unused drawers, shoe boxes under the bed, lining closest, garages and more. I have a small pantry, so I personally put overflow items at the bottom. I have a cabinet for my stockpile of pasta goods, sauces, pickles, jelly, canned vegetables and condiments. My laundry room has several shelves just big enough to store laundry soap, cleaners, paper towels and toilet tissue. My cabinets under my bathroom sinks carry toothpaste, shampoo, body washes, razors and more. I keep my stockpile spread out in several rooms all over the house. You don't need one devoted room for your stockpile. If you do have an extra room, than make sure it's dry and free of any moister.
Keep in mind as well that rodents and bugs love to eat stockpiles. Sometimes your garage or basement may not be a good choice. Also try to arrange your food products by expiration date. Keep the oldest to the front. Try to rotate out your food items otherwise you will have wasted food and money.

Stockpiling vs. hording; I've heard this term thrown around a lot. I want to point out the differences in hording and stockpiling. Hording is when someone collects items that they "think" they're going to use but NEVER do. Stockpiling is buying items that you "will" use and will replenish once used.

Your stockpile should never collect dust. I know that there are some Extreme Couponers that collect items they may never use or have such a HUGE stockpile that you see rows and rows of toilet paper, but those are far and few in-between a true couponer. I enjoy my stockpile and adding to it. But my family can eat and use up everything I buy up pretty fast too!

I would also recommend getting a deep freezer if you can. I purchased a nice 5.0 cubic foot freezer to store in my garage. This is great to use when you purchase bulk meat or frozen food items you find on sale. I have around 40lbs of fresh chicken breast I purchased from a local farm. It was much cheaper than store bought. Your freezer is like your backup grocery store. If I run out of butter, milk, waffles or anything else, I just head to the garage and not the store. You will be surprised at what you can freeze. It's great for storing large pizzas, tons of frozen vegetables, loaves of bread, ice cream and meats. Your stockpile is your saving grace. It's to help you save money at the store along with the coupons you use.

15 CHAPTER -What is Coupon Fraud?

Coupon fraud is using a coupon for any other way that it's intended use. Coupons are a federally regulated industry. That is good news for the consumer because the language on the coupon must be specific. If the coupon states used for ANY product from a line of products, that means ANY and not just the product pictured. If the language states you can only use this coupon once per transaction that means you can only use that coupon for that transaction at checkout. You can't use two of the same coupons. If the coupon states a certain size or product, you are only allowed to purchase that product in that size.

People make mistakes and you may not notice that you grabbed the wrong product. The cash register will reject the coupon and the cashier will probably ask if you grabbed the right product. Knowingly using a coupon towards a product for which it was not intended is coupon fraud and is punishable by federal law.

Another type of coupon fraud is copying coupons. You cannot copy any type of coupon for any reason. You cannot copy printed coupons, store coupons or Catalina coupons.

Selling coupons is another form of coupon fraud. Selling coupons by auction or any other form is against federal regulations. Coupon clipping services offer coupons to be sold but claim they are charging you for only processing and cutting the coupons. These disclaimers are not legally binding. Such invalid disclaimers serve to prove that the seller/auctioneer knows that their illicit coupon sales are inappropriate and subject to civil and/or criminal penalties. This is a fine line of coupon fraud and if you choose to use a coupon service or start a coupon service you are taking a risk.

The worst form of coupon fraud is to produce and/or use a fake coupon. It's hard today to spot counterfeit money, almost as hard to spot a fake coupon. The Penalties for those convicted of coupon fraud can be up to 17 years with a penalty of $5 million. You may even get a prison sentence of three to five years. Financial penalties generally vary, but have often been in excess of $200,000.
So what do you do to protect yourself?

Coupons that have high values on them could possibly be a counterfeit coupon. If it's too good to be true, then is probably is. High values coupons are rare and you can only trust a high value coupon if it came from the manufacture.

Check the expiration date. If the expiration date is longer than a few months, this could possibly be a counterfeit coupon or they do not have an expiration date listed. Only trust coupons that you have clipped from your local newspaper from your local store or from the manufacture.

Many fake coupons do not have a UPC code. This is a HUGE red flag. All coupons have a UPC code on them. Store coupons are the exception. Store coupons print a unique code for only that store. This is usually located on the bottom or top of the coupon. Bar codes are also changing to prevent fraud. You may have noticed two different bar codes on your coupons. The GS1 Data Bar Coupon Format is a new format will provide manufacturers more options for purchase requirements and values and make it possible to code more complex offers. This code may even help stop fraudulent coupons.

Be careful of coupons that are sent to you by email. PDF coupons can be easily manipulated and changed. Not all PDF's are counterfeit, but look at the source of where that coupon came from.

If your friend sends you a link to a coupon kindly explain that you may not be allowed to use that coupon. Manufactures only send coupons to the subscriber. It's only allowed to forward that coupon if it states this in the email. Normally there is a link and you are only allowed to print that coupon twice. If you can print multiple times, this could be a red flag to a fake coupon.

The best rule of thumb to protect yourself is trust your sources. Be informed and keep your eyes open. Stores make a profit off of coupons. If we allowed to use fake coupons the stores will lose money and stop accepting coupons altogether.

If you suspect a coupon is a fake, you can visit The Coupon Information Corporation (CIC) for a list of current fraudulent coupons or contact me and I will try to assist you.

Coupon Information Corporation
Tel (703) 684-5307

16 CHAPTER Couponing Etiquette 101

With today's economy, more and more people are turning to coupons to help save money. Every day I walk into my store I see more customers with binders and coupon holders than ever before. With couponing, you need to know and understand coupon etiquette.

Coupon Etiquette is to teach you the unspoken rules of couponing (which will keep you from being disliked in the coupon community). When you are polite and respectful to your cashier and management, you will typically be able to resolve questions and issues they may have with regards to coupons. Have your coupons organized prior to handing over to the cashier. Have ALL FREE coupons such as BOGO FREE ones together. Smile and be polite to your cashier and other consumers. Being courteous to others goes a long way and your cashiers will love and remember you for it.

Shelf clearing is frowned upon with fellow couponers. What I mean by shelf clearing is purchasing 10 to 20 sale items and not leaving any product left for other consumers to purchase. Sometimes shelves are empty for legitimate reasons: the store did not order enough stock because they did not anticipate a high demand, there was limited supply available and the stores could only get the small amount, or someone simply needed a large amount for a party or community/church function. If you shop the first day of the sale and buy all or most of the products on the shelf you are a shelf-clearer. You are not a shelf-clearer if you go to the store and there is only 1 product on the shelf and you buy it.

You are not a shelf-clearer if there are a significant number of products on the shelf and you buy a large quantity that does not come close to clearing the shelf. If you need to purchase a large amount of items, call your store manager ahead of time. They can pull the product for you and have it set off to the side for you're to purchase.

Don't be a peelie or blinkie thief. A peelie is a free coupon that you will find a product. A blinkie is a machine that spits out a coupon for you to use in your grocery store isle. When you see peelies on a product it's intended for you to purchase that product first before using the free coupon to use at the register or for later. Please do not peel off and take all those coupons, which are considered stealing. When you see a blinkie, those are intended for you to take, but only a few. Take one or two, but please leave the rest for everyone else to enjoy.

Don't steal your neighbors coupon inserts or take coupon inserts out of newspapers without paying for them. Only paying for one, but taking several newspapers from the self-serve newspaper vending machines is frowned upon. Another example is taking the inserts out of newspapers without buying the paper. Lastly, driving by houses and taking the newspapers from the driveways without asking the owner's permission is not a good way to find coupons. Most of these examples are in one way or another form of stealing.

Use the coupon as it was intended for. What I mean by this is if a coupon says "any" then you can truly buy ANY of those products. If it says good on only "2 -4 oz." then you must buy that size.

If a coupon is for a specific variety or flavor, then that is what you must purchase indicated on the coupon. Manufacturer's usually put a picture of their newest or most expensive product on the coupon to make you think that is what you have to buy. The picture is not always the case. The wording on the coupon is the final say in what you must purchase. Last but not lease, do not use expired coupons. If you mistakenly use one, that is fine. If you intended on using several expired coupons, than that is a form of fraud.

Lastly, pass up the freebies if you don't need or use them. We all know the show Extreme Couponing. In the show they have couponers scoop up all kinds of freebies just because they can! On the show, one lady comes to mind. She purchased 50 bags or more of cat treats and doesn't even own a cat! This is just wrong and greedy in my book. If you intend on giving those cat treats to your local shelter, then you have a reason to purchase those freebies. If not, pass up the freebies. Someone else may need them. Using coupons is a benefit that manufacturer's provide to us, not a right. Manufacturers release coupons on certain varieties of their products for a reason, they want to sell that particular item. It's very important that we abide by these rules. If we don't follow the rules, manufactures may stop offering coupons to consumers.

17 CHAPTER -How to Coupon at Walgreen's

Learning how to coupon doesn't stop at your local grocery store. Did you know you can stock up on cheap or free items at your local drug store? Drug stores like Walgreens, CVS and Rite Aid offer coupons, reward points, monthly deals and coupon books to provide customers incentives to come and shop.

Couponing at your local drug store can be a little more intimidating than at your local grocery store. While couponing at all three can provide great deals, you may want to start out with one first. Walgreens is my drug store of choice for the following examples. Walgreens is many times referred to as Wags when fellow couponers "talk coupon".

You will learn many terms and abbreviations when you start to coupon. Another term at Walgreens is RR, it means Register Rewards. Register Rewards are like coupons that print out at the register that you can use like money. They are triggered by certain products that you purchase only at Walgreens. It's very similar to Catalina coupons. There are rules to using RR, but can give you the BEST discount when combining with coupons. Another NEW term is BR or Balance Rewards. You will need to sign up at your local Walgreens to join. With this program you start collecting points to earn point towards cash rewards. For instance, if you collect 5,000 points your reward is $5.00. The more points you earn, the more you can redeem. This is a new incentive program that just came out within the past year. I'm going to give you some examples and scenarios to help you better understand how this works. Once you get the hang of it, you'll be a Walgreens shopping pro!

For the working mom like myself, I head over to my favorite blog and see what deals are in store for this week. They usually have a breakdown of RR Deals, BR Deals, Grocery, Pharmacy and maybe another category. To make things easier for me and to save time, my favorite grocery blog has put together scenarios for me. I just print them out, find my coupons and shop! If you don't have a favorite blog yet, you can still create your own scenarios with some examples I'm going to put together for you.

For this example I'm going to say this week we have Lipton Tea on sale for $1.00. Walgreens is offering a $1.00 RR when you buy one tea. That's basically like getting it for free. This is a great item to start out with. Next we have $10 in RR wyb Estroven PM caplets, 24 ct, $10.00. I also have coupons for both products.

Transaction #1
Sale items:
$1 RR wyb Lipton Tea varieties, 18.5oz- $1.00
$10 in RR wyb Estroven PM Caplets, 24 ct, $10.00
Purchase:
(1) Lipton Tea, 18.5oz- $1.00
(1) Estroven PM Caplets, 24ct-$10.00
-Use: $0.25/1 Lipton tea coupon
-Use: $5.00 off Estroven nighttime item
Total Due: $5.75
Get Back: $11 in RR (Register Rewards) ($1.00 RR and a $10.00 RR)

But the fun is not over yet! You have $11.00 to spend towards another purchase. You can either save your RR for another time or start another transaction on the same day.

For this example I'm doing a same day transaction. In this next transaction, Hefty Waste bags have a BR deal. Get 1,000 BR when you buy one bag. Goody's also has $1.50 RR when you buy any Goody's product for $2.99.

Transaction #2
Sale items:
1,000 BR wyb Hefty Waste Bags, any variety, $5.99
$1.50 RR when you buy any Goody's product for $2.99
Purchase
(1) Hefty Waste Bags, $5.99
(1) Gallon Whole Milk-$3.49
(1) Goody Ouchless Elastics, 27 ct $2.99
(1) Colgate Optic White Toothpaste, 4oz $2.99
(1) Speed Stick $2.50
-Use $1.00 off Colgate Optic White toothpaste, SS 1/13
-Use $1.25 off Lady Speed stick product, SS 1/13
-Use $0.50 off 1 Goody Ouchless product, printable
-Use your $10 RR
Total Due: $5.21

Plus you earned 1,000 BR points and $2.50 RR to use for your next transaction.

Rule #1: You need to have more product than coupons. In the transaction above the milk and the Hefty bags did not have manufacture coupons. Register Rewards are considered coupons. When using both manufacture and store coupons, hand the cashier your manufacture coupons first, then your Walgreens store coupons. This will prevent the register from beeping a coupon overage. Each coupon has to link to a product.

When you have more coupons than products you need a filler item. "Filler" is any inexpensive item. Great options are candies, gum, pencils or clearance merchandise

. There is an exception to this rule mentioned above: Walgreens coupons DO NOT affect your coupon to product ratio. You can use as many of them as needed at check out.

For both transactions mentioned above, you purchased $28.96 worth of items. With coupons and RR coupons you spent out of pocket $10.96, earned 1,000 BR points and $1.50RR. You can keep going and going with these kinds of transactions. You want to make sure you use your RR before they expire. For your BR points, you want to earn as much as you can and utilized the points for larger purchases.

Rule #2: If you purchase more than one of the same RR participating item per transaction, you will only receive one RR-NOT two. In order to get more than one RR coupon when purchasing more than one of the same qualifying items, you need to make separate transactions. You can purchase different RR promotions on the same transaction and receive more than one RR at the time of checkout.

Rule #3: Register Rewards deals do NOT roll. This means that if you receive a $3RR for purchasing a package of paper towels, you cannot use this same RR to purchase another package of paper towels and expect another RR to be generated.

Another great reason to shop Walgreens is their BOGO sales! As I mentioned before in the eBook how I love BOGO sales, you will love Walgreens even more. They allow you to use a BOGO coupon with a BOGO sale! What does that mean? Means you can get both items for FREE! Check with your Walgreens coupon policy which states,

"When items are featured in a Buy One, Get One Free promotion, up to two coupons can be used against the items being purchased, as long as the net price does not go below zero for the items being purchased".

Keep an eye out for clearance tags! There are two kinds of tags you need to look for. Orange tags are from the corporate office and you can find them at any Walgreens. Yellow tags are specific to that store. You can often pair up manufacture coupons and Walgreen coupons and score free items!

Walgreen sales start every Sunday and run through the week. As a working mom, I find the best time is shopping early Sunday morning when the store opens. Walgreens has limited stock on their shelves unlike grocery stores. They only stock up a few times per week. You can ask your local Walgreens what days they stock items on the shelves. Most Walgreens are open late as well. This can give you an advantage to sales when they stock the day before.

18 CHAPTER In Conclusion

Couponing has and always will change the way I shop. Even with our money situation getting better, I still have a hard time not using coupons. There are days I just run into the grocery store without my coupons. It happens. I make it a general rule to try and use my coupons as much as I can. There have been times I stopped couponing "hard core" and just used up my stockpile. You never know when you stockpile will come in handy such as a job loss or a disaster. It's good to have a backup supply of items that can last a long time, such as canned goods and frozen foods.

I encourage you to find coupon blogs in your city or state and read them. There are many resources out there to help you learn how to coupon. I hope this book has helped you learn and understand the general rule to couponing. Manage your time, keep organized and remember that you are helping your family save money.

Best of all, you now know the basic skills on becoming an Extreme Couponer!

Good Luck and Have Fun!!

ABOUT THE AUTHOR

I started couponing in February 2011. Couponing couldn't have come at a better time in my life. In January, my husband lost all of his overtime and pay-period deductions had increased greatly by law. Add to that an increase in healthcare spending due to a couple of diagnosed chronic illnesses and we lost over $15,000 of income within a few months. We needed to drastically cut back on our spending. At that time, our grocery bill was around $800.00 per month. We had to make some major changes and fast.

I went online the next day and started researching how to coupon. I learned that my original way of couponing was incorrect and I needed to change the way I shop. Several months later, I started saving over 50% of my grocery bill and brought home more food and products than I could ever imagine! I save anywhere from 50% to 90% of my grocery bill every week! In this economy you can save money and get your family back on track. After one year of couponing, I saved my family $4,800! Couponing can fit into anyone's lifestyle. You just need to know the right tools to succeed

Jennifer E Clark *has been an artist, writer, website designer, avid blogger and couponer for many years. Jennifer is a full-time working mom of one little boy and two teenage step-daughters. When she's not working she's at home taking care of her children and husband. She also runs "Mixed Nuts Mommy". She is currently working on a Children's Book due to release this year.*

www.ingramcontent.com/pod-product-compliance
Lightning Source LLC
Chambersburg PA
CBHW071755200526
45167CB00018B/2071